CW00520300

# The Offensive

Bleaux Savage

Copyright Page

Front cover photo by Frankie Lopez on Unsplash
Back cover photo by Antoine Rault on Unsplash

# CONTENTS

# INTRODUCTION

We are an army of the light called to pursue the darkness.

The Lord is raising up an army who understands warfare. An army of spiritual huntsmen who are not afraid to pursue the enemies of God into the darkness.
We can fight in the dark because we are the light. (Matthew 5:14)

# 1. THE HUNTSMAN

**WEAPON: OFFENSIVE STRATEGIES**

**"You are the light of the world. [...]" - Matthew 5:14, NKJV.**

## WE ARE THE LIGHT

Satan and his demons operate in the darkness and lurk in the shadows as unlawful occupants. We are not called to fight men but to fight the unseen evil in this world. We are an army of the light called to pursue the darkness.

God wants us to be the pursuers not the pursued. The Lord is raising up an army who understands warfare. An army of spiritual huntsmen who are not afraid to pursue the enemies of God into the darkness. We can fight in the dark because we are the light (Matthew 5:14). The enemy operates in the unseen. God wants His people to be unafraid to go into the unseen. In this Kingdom Age the Lord is bringing the prophetic seer gift to the forefront. Through this gift God exposes plots of the enemy that once went unseen. We are called to pursue and to overtake the darkness.

We must stop waiting for the enemy to come to our house before we engage. It's time to go to his house and plunder it! We must send the hosts of heaven to destroy the enemy's hiding places in the spirit realm. Yes, the kingdom of darkness has hiding places from where they plan and launch attacks. They are not hidden from God. We are in a time where the Lord is showing His people these hidden plans and places. Do not be surprised if you hear conversations or see plans of what the enemy is plotting. It is our commission to destroy them, to drive them out, and to establish the Kingdom (Numbers 33:52; 2 Corinthians 10:4). There is no neutral ground. The territory either belongs to the kingdom of darkness or to the Kingdom of Light.

# SCHEMATICS

During prayer on October 23, 2021 I saw a map laying on a table. A demon had its hand on the map. The hand was a bony, sinewy, and dead looking hand. As I looked I heard, "The enemy has maps and plans for cities and regions". I felt led to destroy the maps and plans that the demon was laying its hand on. I commanded the maps of the enemy to be destroyed and to be ripped up in the name of Jesus. I also commanded the enemy to be unable to read the maps and plans. As I spoke those words, I saw maps in multiple different places around the country being destroyed. I saw a lower ranking demon holding a map in its hand and screaming because it could no longer read the plan.

As soon as I finished commanding the maps and plans to be destroyed, the first demon with its hand on the map turned and looked at me. I then commanded the hosts of heaven to take down the demon and to protect me, my family, and my home.

I saw a member of the host run into the room where the demon was and rush towards it. Then my ability to see this scene ended.

I felt an immediate shift in the spiritual atmosphere and saw much chaos in the spirit realm. It felt like a frenzy was in the air. The Lord then said to me, "It's time to get in the secret place." I felt an urgency to do so. I knew that the Lord said this to me because you become hidden in the secret place. I sat down and entered the secret place in the Lord. In the secret place the enemy cannot locate you.

As soon as I sat down, an angel of the Lord flew straight through the wall into my living room. The angel stood in front of me and said, "I am a servant of the most high God. I've been sent to protect you." I felt the presence of the Lord immediately over me. However, I did not recognize this particular angel so I still confirmed by asking, "Do you acknowledge that Jesus Christ is the son of God and that He came in the flesh?" The angel said an affirmative "Yes." He stood over me as I hid in the secret place in the Lord and did not leave until the chaos in the spiritual atmosphere subsided.

Whenever you do warfare for the Lord He will always protect you. We are all called to be His huntsmen. There are many people who do not understand this type of warfare because they do not know it exists. Oftentimes, intercessors are engaging in this type of warfare but are unaware.

## NOTHING PRAYERS

I recall one particular time a few years ago when I was driving home from church. I had always felt uncomfortable in my spirit when going down this particular road. I decided to do something about it so I prayed a simple 2 or 3 line prayer commanding any demonic oppression to be lifted from the area. I felt like I had just done absolutely nothing in the spirit realm. I thought, "Well, that didn't do anything." A few moments later while stopped at a red light, I saw a large dragon fall from the sky. Its body landed on the street and its decapitated head rolled across the road. I realized in that moment that the prayers that we think are powerless are anything but.

These seemingly powerless prayers shake the second heaven and bring down powers and rulers of darkness. When you don't think, feel, or sense anything happening - it is. Our voices have the power to shake the heavens and to bring down demonic strongholds. The angels and hosts of heaven are just waiting for us to speak. Don't keep them waiting. They cannot act on their own accord. They are waiting for the Sons of God to arise.

## THE LORD IS THE HUNTSMAN

What is a huntsman? A huntsman is one who pursues the predator. By nature mankind is the highest on the food chain. What gives humans the advantage over a large powerful animal? Weaponry. This is the same way in the spirit realm. We have been given the weapon of our voice and the revelation of His spoken Word.

God acts in the offensive. Before satan ever fell the Lord had already created a righteous army - the hosts of heaven. He always has a plan. Due to our limited perception we don't always see what God is doing. This has caused the belief system that God plays defense. Christ is the lamb slain before the foundation of the world (Revelation 13:8). In other words, the Lord already had a plan in place to defeat Lucifer before he was satan and before man was ever created.

Jesus is the lion of Judah (Revelation 5:5). A lion does not wait for you to attack because a lion is a predator animal. It does the hunting. It is this fighting nature that God is wanting to get into His body. A shift in perception is needed concerning spiritual warfare. There are two sides to warfare. The defensive and the offensive. The church for most of history has been engaging in the defensive only.

What does defense versus offense look like?

- Defense is a reactionary perspective. It waits until the enemy attacks to engage the defenses.
    - In the defensive you are unable to take new territory.
    - Defense mode should not be the default position of warfare for a Christian. This will keep you in a constant state of battle just to maintain what you already have. This is the place where most Christians reside.

- Offense is a Kingdom dominion perspective. It identifies the enemy and wages a detrimental assault with the offensive weapons that are available to us.
    - In the offensive you take territory constantly. Everywhere you go you are taking ground because you bring the Kingdom of God with you.
    - Offense mode should be the default position in warfare. This will keep you constantly taking territory and

advancing the Kingdom. This is the place where God is bringing His church.

When I say "territory" I mean taking authority over the spiritual atmosphere of cities, regions, and nations. This is done by using offensive weapons to push the enemy out of your homes, out of your neighborhoods, out of your schools, and out of your churches.

We are called to be conquerors (Romans 8:37). In the natural, defensive fighting often leaves "defensive wounds" on the individual from blocking their attacker's strikes. This is why Christians often get weary in battle. Christians think satan wants to get into the boxing ring with them and go a round or two. No! The enemy is a murderer - a hitman. A hitman doesn't want to fight you. He wants to eliminate you. Immobilized or dead satan doesn't care as long as you are out of his way. It's time for Christians to take off the boxing gloves and understand that they are not getting into a fist fight with satan. Jesus already took satan down with His death and resurrection. Now our job is to use the authority that Christ has given us to command the enemy's encampments to be torn down. It's time to drive out the unlawful occupants (Luke 10:19; John 14:12).

## Chapter Takeaways:

- God is raising up spiritual huntsmen who tear down the unlawful occupation of darkness over individuals, counties, regions, and nations of the world.
- Offensive spiritual warfare purges the spiritual landscape of demonic activity and operations to take territory for the Kingdom of God.
- Spiritual warfare starts at home. It is knowing that you have the authority to kick the enemy out and to protect your home and family members. It is learning not to tolerate any attack or interference by the enemy whether it be frustration, anger, sadness or stress. So many people

believe living in a state of stress is normal. It is NOT!

- If you are not joyful and at peace in your home, change the spiritual atmosphere. Having a heavenly atmosphere in your home is an easily attainable goal. I say everyday, "I evict all darkness from my home and give no evil spirit any permission to enter my home. I claim my home and property for the Kingdom of God and His operations. My home is a place of the Kingdom of God where the Spirit of God and His angels dwell."
- A spiritual huntsman:
  - Guards their home, guards their family, guards their friends, and guards their coworkers.
  - Does NOT tolerate the enemy or even small daily attacks such as fear, anxiety, anger, and worry. Too many people think they have to tolerate such things or they simply see it as "normal". This is how the enemy keeps you distracted and

worn down to prevent you from fulfilling your destiny.
- Makes their home a place of glory where the enemy cannot enter.
- Is not afraid of the unorthodox and does not need everything to make sense to the natural mind or to conform to a religious framework.
- Is not afraid to invade the darkness because they know that they are the light.
- Tears down the kingdom of darkness by destroying the enemy's encampments. This is offensive warfare that God wants all in the body of Christ to be operating in.
- Expels the demonic and calls down the Kingdom of heaven to earth.
- Makes a habitation for the presence of God and His angels. Places where demons once occupied angels will now occupy.

- We need fresh revelation on warfare for a new Kingdom generation.

- We cannot continue to play defense and think we will accomplish ALL that God has for us in the Kingdom Age.

# 2. FREEDOM WALKERS

"It is for freedom that Christ has set us free. [...]"
- Galatians 5:1, NIV.

## DRIVE OUT THE DARKNESS

**Before we get into our offensive spiritual weapons let's do a quick synopsis. Everything changed after Jesus.** Before Christ came satan held the keys of hell and death. This is why we see perplexing stories such as the summoning of the spirit of Samuel by the witch of Endor (1 Samuel 28:7-20). Jesus now possesses the keys of hell and death (Revelation 1:17-18). The enemy has been operating in pseudo power for the past 2,000 years and trying to keep up the charade even though he no longer has the keys to his own house anymore.

While on the earth Jesus operated in power and authority over demonic spirits. In His resurrection Jesus returned with the keys in hand having stripped the thief of his former spiritual authority that man had surrendered to him at the tree. Now Jesus wants us to operate in the same spiritual authority over demonic spirits. It is our job to remove the spiritual trespassers and to liberate the captives. Christ has entrusted us with this power and He expects us to use it.

Jesus gave me a revelation about the freedom that He walked in while on the earth. He told me, "This is a truth of the Kingdom". He showed me that nowhere in Scripture does it say that Jesus was ever oppressed or attacked by satan. That language is never used in Scripture. Why? Because that is not Kingdom living. We are coming to a place where we will all live like this - untouchable by the enemy. Being untouchable is a choice. Jesus walked in complete and total authority over satan while on the earth. This is how we are supposed to live.

When satan tried to tempt Jesus in the wilderness (Matthew 4:1-11) the moment the Lord told him to leave he had to leave immediately. The enemy was only allowed to talk to Jesus as long as He permitted. There was not a battle, a fight, or any resistance. This is the type of authority that Jesus walked in and this is the type of authority Jesus wants us to walk in. Satan was allowed to stay in Jesus' presence as an example for us of how to exercise our authority. This encounter was for our edification.

The serpent came to tempt the second Adam in the same way he had tempted the first and succeeded. The second Adam overcame where the first failed. The enemy will only be allowed to attempt something as long as we permit his attempt. We do not have to accept or tolerate the enemy or any assault ever. Period. To accept anything else is to live subpar Christianity.

# JESUS IS OUR EXAMPLE OF FREEDOM

It is time for the church to become the predator and to no longer be the prey. Jesus walked in total victory over the enemy. He is the example of freedom we are to follow, not our experiences. Jesus expects us to literally walk all over the devil. "I have given you authority to trample on snakes and scorpions and to overcome all the power of the enemy; nothing will harm you." - Luke 10:19, NIV. This verse is a reference to ground dwelling demon spirits that reside on the earth. It is not just figurative language.

When Jesus walked the earth demons started screaming and begging not to be harmed by Him (Luke 4:41). They were in dread and fear of Him. We must walk as Christ walked where the enemy was too afraid to attack Him. When we walk into the room demons should run out and be too afraid to return. This is the type of power that God expects His church to walk in. Jesus didn't pay for subpar Christianity.

As long as we believe that we are called to fight and to wrestle with satan we will live in a state of constant battle and defeat. The enemy creates a false scenario where he makes you think that you have to fight with him. This is to wear us out. Command him to leave, don't ask him to leave! Remember, Christ cast out demons with a single word (Matthew 8:16) not with screaming and travailing. Why do Christians have trouble getting rid of or casting out demons? Because they don't believe that they can cast them out just like Christ did. Jesus said that if we believe we can do what He did and greater (John 14:12). To believe otherwise is false theology. False theology that has entered the church because the enemy knows all it takes is a single word to remove him. Satan encountered Christ so he knows what level of authority has been given to us.

# SPIRITUAL ATTACKS ARE NOT A BADGE OF HONOR

Our measure of success is not based upon the enemy's actions. It is based upon Christ. Many Christians have a backwards perception and think that if the enemy is attacking them then that is an automatic sign of progress. The enemy will always be your enemy and attack whenever he can but some people wear it like a badge of honor. Christians have to some degree "religi-fied" spiritual assaults from the enemy. This belief has caused Christians to tolerate constant spiritual attacks when they don't have to and to even justify them as a "normal" part of daily life.

**Chapter Takeaways:**

- **Jesus walked in complete and total freedom while on the earth. We must understand that Jesus changed everything for us.**

- Jesus is our example of freedom and the model for the Christian life not our experiences.
- Jesus cast out demons with a single word spoken with authority. We have been given power to do the same. We have to believe we have it and use it!
- We are not called to wrestle with the devil but to drive him out using the authority that Christ has given us.
- Stop fighting a defeated enemy!

# 3. SPEAK

WEAPON: THE WORDS WE SPEAK

"Death and life are in the power of the tongue
[...]" - Proverbs 18:21, NASB.

**Let's talk weaponry.** What exactly are our
weapons? The Word and the words that we speak.

# BE OFFENSIVE

The armor of God is made up of 5 pieces of
defensive armor and 1 offensive weapon - the
Sword of the Spirit which is the Word of God.
These are the 6 pieces that make up the armor of
God (Ephesians 6:13-17). There are six pieces for
man because the number of mankind is 6
(Revelation 13:18).

1. Belt of Truth

2. Breastplate of Righteousness
3. Feet fitted with the Gospel
4. Shield of Faith
5. Helmet of Salvation
6. Sword of the Spirit

The church is very familiar with the armor of God so I'm not going to go over the defensive aspects, only the offensive weapon. The Sword of the Spirit is the only offensive weapon mentioned in Ephesians. We must know the Word of God to wield the Sword correctly.

One day while sitting in my office at work I saw a full suit of armor fly across the room towards me. I later told my mother. She said to me, "I was praying for the armor of God to be on you." **The armor of God is an actual spiritual armor**. It is not just figurative language that Paul devised.

## WORDS ARE SPIRIT

Words are the most powerful thing in existence. With our words we invite the God who created the cosmos into our very being. The spoken word can literally draw the God of heaven. With our words confession is made unto salvation (Romans 10:10).

What do words do in the spirit realm?
- They create or destroy.
- They help or hinder.
- They move or halt.
- They accelerate or delay.
- They prosper or rob.
- They bless or curse.
- They bring faith or doubt.
- They bring healing or sickness.
- They encourage or shame.
- They open or they close.
- They decide life or death.

Words determine our destiny. Words can shift nations. Words are spirit.

The Word of God does not stand still. Words move forward and create what was spoken in the spirit realm. What is created in the spirit realm eventually happens in the natural realm. This is why the enemy is always trying to influence what we think and say. The spiritual influences and creates what is physical. From the spiritual realm God spoke the natural realm into existence. We know from creation itself that God's words (spiritual) created the world (natural realm) (Psalm 33:6).

The Lord showed me years ago that words and even thoughts and emotions are spiritual in origin. 2 Corinthians 4:18, NKJV says: "[...] For the things which are seen *are* temporary, but the things which are not seen *are* eternal." Spoken words can be felt and heard but remain unseen. Words are spiritual and therefore affect both the spiritual and natural realms simultaneously.

There are only 2 spiritual kingdoms in operation. Our words either originate from God's Kingdom or from the adversary's kingdom. Words either disperse the enemy or invite him. When we speak the enemy's words we come into verbal agreement with his ideas. This gives him something to use.

The enemy has worked to install his words into our everyday vocabulary. Even some of the things we find funny are subtle ways to get us to compromise. For example: "My children never listen!", "It's normal for teenagers to be rebellious.", "I'm dying for a piece of cake.", "My feet are killing me!", "I'm losing my mind.", "I'm so stupid.", "I'm having a bad day.", I'm so stressed out!", "Oh my gosh, I'm so OCD!", "Wow, you're old!", "Things don't work like they used to...", and "I'm having a senior moment." When we speak words we are coming into agreement with those words. Words are alive and will do what they have been spoken to do. It is a spiritual law.

When we speak God's words we come into agreement with Him and give Him access to move in our lives. During your prayer time include declarations and make them something that you do as a normal part of your day. I make declarations morning, afternoon, or evening -

wherever I feel I need to. I see great results by doing this. Also, worship is very important. When you worship you change the spiritual atmosphere around you. Portals to heaven will actually open when you worship. There have been times when I have seen the Father on His throne in heaven while worshiping in my living room. This happens when all people worship and is not reserved for the few.

- Making daily declarations is very important.
- When we make declarations we should not just be reciting words. We should be engaging both our soul and our spirit in what we are saying.
- Declarations open portals in the spirit realm on your behalf to bring blessings into your life. They also activate angels to work on your behalf.
- Declaring the truth also removes the demonic because demons do not want to hear truth spoken.
- Declarations are taking God's Word and personalizing it for our own life.

- When you declare God's Word you come into alignment with His promises.
- Declaration examples:
  The Word says in 2 Timothy 1:7, NKJV: "For God has not given us a spirit of fear, but of power and of love and of a sound mind." I can either recite this verse or put it in my own words. "Thank you Lord that you have removed a spirit of fear from my life and have given me your fearless spirit, your authority, your heart for others, and the mind of Christ." It is about taking God's Word and personalizing it for your situation.
- Let's choose our words wisely.

**Note: If you ever feel frustrated during your prayer time, it may be because it is time to go to the next level. Jesus is always doing something. When Jesus takes a step forward and we do not discern His movements, it can cause us to not be able to hear Him or feel Him like we normally do. How do you fix this? Tell the Lord you are ready to go to the next level. What you are doing is taking a step forward in the spirit realm and**

getting back in sync with Jesus. When you do this you will be able to hear and feel Him more clearly again because you are now where He is.

# WORDS ARE VISIBLE IN THE SPIRIT REALM

Words are not visible in the physical realm but can be seen in the spiritual realm by spiritual beings. Angels are spiritual beings and can see the Word of the Lord as it is spoken out of His mouth and out of ours. Psalm 103:20, NKJV says: Bless the Lord, you His angels, Who excel in strength, who do His word, Heeding the voice of His word." Angels DO His word. Angels move on the Word of the Lord. These words must be spoken by either God or by one of His images on the earth in order to be executed.

Demons can also see words that people speak. This is why the enemy doesn't want the Word of God spoken; he can see the Word of God moving and creating in the spirit realm. The enemy needs your mouth in order to exact his plans. This is why the enemy tries to get people to speak negative things against their assignment or other people's destinies. Our adversary does not have the authority as a spirit being to enact his desires in the physical realm. One who has authority in the physical realm must speak it. God gave us both physical and spiritual bodies because we are designed to reign in both realms. This is why we are created from the dust of the earth. We are made from the dust of the earth because we are made to rule over it. **We are the only creatures in all of God's creation that operate and are made to rule in both the spiritual and physical realms simultaneously.**

On multiple occasions I have seen people's words as they were spoken out of their mouths. They look like streams of water. Words spoken from Holy Spirit's influence look different from words that are spoken under the enemy's influence or from human opinion. Proverbs 18:4, NKJV says, "The words of a man's mouth *are* deep waters [..]" God is talking about something literal in the spirit realm. He is not using fancy figurative language.

Sometimes I will literally see words written on people. One day I saw a man with the word "deceptive" written across his face. I knew that this word was written on him because he deceived people. Years ago I saw a man with the words "sex offender" written on his chest. I later looked up the area's sex offender registry and found his picture listed. Not long ago I saw the word "trustworthy" written across the chest of a man in my church. Another time I looked over across the church sanctuary and saw words written over a woman's head in an arc. The words said that the Lord was pleased with her. I later found out that the Lord had just told her to do something and she had been obedient.

# MANIPULATION OF SPIRITUAL LAW

When a demon uses the words of someone who is speaking evil or ill against you - this is called witchcraft. Much of what witches/warlocks do is practice the spiritual truth of speaking to affect the natural world. Except they are not using God's will or Word to do so. Instead, they are either speaking their own will or the will of a demon spirit. This is manipulation of spiritual law. Witchcraft is warping the laws of the spirit realm and using them for the purposes of the kingdom of darkness. Other versions of this are called "manifesting" or "law of attraction".

## BUILDING IN THE SPIRIT

When we speak in tongues we actually build and create things in the spirit realm. This is why the enemy hates it so much and comes against this gift so strongly. I remember one particular time where I saw a woman in church speaking in tongues. As she spoke, objects were coming out of her mouth and being created in the spirit realm. I knew that whatever she was speaking was very important and that she was creating something in the spiritual realm. 1 Corinthians 14:4, NIV says: "Anyone who speaks in a tongue edifies themselves [...]". The word "edifies" is the Greek word *oikodomeo*. It has the meaning of "to construct", "to build", or "to build a house".[1] Scripture is telling us that speaking in tongues builds and constructs.

When we are baptized in the Holy Spirit the fire of God literally rests upon our heads just like on Pentecost. When I received the gift of tongues I was 9 years old in a boring church service on a Sunday morning. I kept waiting for the service to be over as we were only part way through the singing. All of a sudden the Lord told me to lift my hand. I didn't want anyone to see me so I didn't do it. The Lord kept urging me to do it so I finally lifted my left hand up by my side. As soon as I did, I saw fire rushing towards me from across the sanctuary. The fire hit the top of my head. My jaw felt like it was on fire and I instantly began speaking in tongues. Never underestimate the power of a boring church service. Jesus shows up there too.

## HOW TO WIELD THE SWORD

Speaking with authority is part of what makes us in God's image. Our God is a King. With His voice He commands the heavens and earth to be formed. With His voice He commands the rising and falling of nations. Our voices are like deep waters (Proverbs 18:4) but His voice is like the sound of many waters (Ezekiel 1:24). Because we are made in His image we have a likeness of His authority.

Our weapon is the Word. The Word is Christ Himself (John 1:1,14). This means that the sword is verbal in nature. We are kings and priests before our God (Revelation 5:10) who serve under the King of kings and the Great High Priest. A king rules and commands by speaking. We are called to operate as kings in the spirit realm by tearing down the kingdom of darkness and building the Kingdom of God just like our Father in heaven does. Using the sword is not just quoting verses at demons and hoping that they leave. <u>Jesus quoted Scripture to satan in the wilderness but he did not leave until he was commanded to.</u>

Quoting Scripture alone is not enough if you don't understand the Word and the power behind what you are speaking. We must have revelation on the Word and the weapons that the Lord has provided to us within it. This takes not just reading but studying the Word and allowing our spirits to understand what is being said.

Satan is a fallen being. Just like an unsaved person the enemy cannot understand the Scriptures or gain revelation. Satan does not understand prophecy. This is why he comes so strongly against the prophetic. He wants everything to be brought into and kept in the realm of facts and logic because that is what he can understand. This is why the enemy also works so hard through theology and religion to philosophize the Bible in order to lessen its revelatory value.

# REVELATION AND THE WORD

Speaking the Word of God is extremely important. However, offensive warfare is much more than just quoting Bible verses at demons. Demons can attend church services and hear Biblical teaching - they may just not like the sounds of it. Satan knows the Gospel.

I have seen demons enter into the church after the Word has been given. They looked like a pack of wolves on the hunt looking side to side for who they could prey upon. This is what Jesus was talking about in Mark 4:14-15, NKJV: "The sower sows the word. And these are the ones by the wayside where the word is sown. When they hear, Satan comes immediately and takes away the word that was sown in their hearts." Many of the things in Scripture that we think are metaphorical are actually literal things happening in the spirit realm. As soon as I saw the demons, I commanded them to leave in the name of Jesus and they left.

This is the type of authority that Christ expects us to be operating in on a normal daily basis.

Practical and tactical application of the Sword of the Spirit is understanding how to apply the Word and use what resources are available to you. We must understand what the Word teaches about how the spirit realm operates and how to command the army of heaven to fight the darkness. The area where we lack revelation is where the enemy operates and creates strongholds. Why? Because wherever the Kingdom of God does not reside the kingdom of darkness will occupy. Our enemy operates in our ignorance.

## HOW TO WEAPONIZE YOUR WORDS

Once the word of God becomes revelation it becomes a weapon to use in our arsenal against the darkness. If we don't understand what we are speaking then we are just waving our sword around in the air not knowing how to use it. This isn't about having a photographic memory and being able to recite Scripture. You can memorize and be able to recite the entire Bible but have zero revelation or practical application of how to use it. Remember, satan quoted Scripture to Christ. Even the devil can recite the Word so that is not what this is about. It is about understanding the power and revelation of each passage of Scripture and how we can use it for each particular situation. For example, I know that because of Psalm 103 that angels act on the word of God. How can I use this information? I am being told a truth about the operations of the spirit realm. When I speak the Word I activate the angels of God. There are many nuggets in Scripture that tell you how things operate.

## REAL LIFE EXAMPLES

You can use words to bless yourself or to curse yourself and those around you. The words you speak affect your life. When you feel and think negatively about yourself and then speak these words the enemy doesn't even have to attack you because you are attacking yourself. Words like "I'm not good enough", "I'm a loser", or "I'm not making an impact". Satan knows if he can get you to speak badly over yourself and your life his job is done. You will eventually believe what you say. The enemy wants you to think that your words have no power when they actually carve out your destiny. Your words either give or revoke permission.

Too many Christians are sin conscious and speak negatively about themselves and speak it over themselves. This is why so many people in the world succeed and Christians don't. Christians will say, "I'm healed" and then turn around and tell everyone about their sickness. Then they do not understand why they are not receiving their healing. When parents say things like "Well, you know teenagers. They are rebellious", etc. they are speaking a curse over their own child. When people say things like "I'm old" or "I'm over the hill" they are inviting death, aging, and disease. We have to be conscious that every word we speak holds power. Words stay in the spirit realm until they fulfill themselves. This is why we must cancel bad and wrong words spoken.

## Chapter Takeaways:

- Words are spiritual. Words are how you reign in the spirit realm.
- With our voices we speak the will of God and His Word. When we speak the truth of His word and will in the earth we allow angels to act.
- Both angels and demons act on the spoken word. In the spirit realm battles are won and lost based upon what we speak.
- God is a King. A king's authority is in their voice. When God speaks His words go out to create what He spoke. Because we are made in God's image and are kings in the

earth we also reign by what we speak
(Revelation 5:10).

- God's Kingdom is built upon His spoken
  Word and the enactment of His will by His
  children.
- The kingdom of darkness is also built by
  the spoken word. We must be careful
  what we speak because whatever we
  speak we give permission to.
- We have both a physical and a spiritual
  body because we are designed to reign in
  both realms. God gave the earth to His
  children.
- We are the only creatures in all of God's
  creation that operate and are made to rule
  in both the spiritual and physical realms
  simultaneously.

# 4. THE SPIRITUAL LANDSCAPE

**WEAPON: UNDERSTANDING THE OPERATIONS OF THE SPIRIT REALM**

**"'The secret things belong to the Lord our God, but the things revealed belong to us and to our children forever [...]'" - Deuteronomy 29:29, NIV.**

**The Lord is always revealing His mysteries to those who listen.** He often reveals the enemy's plots and plans to His seers and prophets. These are not the only people who He reveals this to but He often uses these people to aid the body. The seat of a seer or a prophet allows them to view the enemy's plans through the eyes of Christ. When we see through Him we are able to put things in proper perspective and focus. The enemy should never be the focus. Only Christ and His Kingdom should be the focus (Matthew 6:33).

**Resource: An excellent resource on seers and prophets is** *The Seer Dimensions: Activating Your Prophetic Sight to See the Unseen* **by Jennifer LeClaire.**

Everywhere we go whether we know it, feel it, sense it, hear it, or see it there is a spiritual world in operation. Everyday when we walk into restaurants, shopping centers, airports, or people's homes we are walking into a spiritual atmosphere. Each person also has their own spiritual atmosphere. The physical environments we go into are influenced by the spiritual world around them.

The physical world is wrapped around the spiritual one. The spiritual realm is the original realm. Psalm 102:25-26, NKJV says, "Of old You laid the foundation of the earth, And the heavens *are* the work of Your hands. They will perish, but You will endure; Yes, they will all grow old like a garment; Like a cloak You will change them, And they will be changed."

Even if someone does not see in the spirit realm they will often sense a shift in the spiritual atmosphere. The most common feeling people will have when a demon spirit is near them is fear. The fear you are experiencing is not your own fear. It is important to understand this. What you are feeling is the atmosphere of hell. Demons bring hell's atmosphere with them and angels bring the presence of heaven. If you ever experience this fear immediately command the demon to leave in the authority of Jesus and to never return.

# LAYING THE GROUNDWORK

Often ministers and evangelists struggle to make an impact in particular regions or cities because the spiritual groundwork has not been laid first. We have to understand that the spiritual atmosphere must be conquered first before we can take it for the Kingdom of God. When Christians go into a place without first clearing out the spiritual atmosphere by evicting the powers of darkness that reside in regions, cities, and states we will face more push back and conflict than we should. Some of the warfare we experience is unnecessary but because of wrong theology we think we have to endure it.

When we send the hosts of heaven before us the enemy is removed allowing us to lay the groundwork for the Kingdom. Just like the human heart - a city or a region must be tilled to remove the weeds that have grown up there. We could view the enemy like an invasive species which is not native to the region and seeks to overtake the natural inhabitants. The Kingdom of God is the natural environment of the earth. We must change our mindset to see things as they should be. The earth is meant and designed to be a mirror that reflects that glory of heaven which is the Father's house (Hebrews 8:5).

# TIME

Part of understanding the spiritual realm is understanding time. The physical world is built upon the spiritual world. Prayers can move back and forth across time. Because words are spiritual they are not bound to the physical laws. Prayers and declarations can move through the spiritual landscape into a particular physical point in time.

When I was a child God pulled me outside of time and showed me things that would be happening in the centuries to come. This encounter gave me a better understanding of not only the operations of the physical and spiritual worlds but it also showed me God's perspective on time. When God showed me future events I knew that my life had already been completed and that I was just living it out in the natural realm like a clock on a countdown. The past, the present, and the future are all one to Him because He operates from the highest dimension.

What is happening in the physical world has already happened and is finished in the eyes of God because He is outside of time. Time comes and flows from the Father because He is the author of time and is not bound by what He has created. This is why the enemy often plays with characterizations such as "father time" because he has seen the Father seated on His throne and time coming from His being. He is the Beginning and the End. The Alpha and the Omega. The First and the Last.

All of history has already unfolded before the Father's eyes; this is how Jesus is the lamb slain before the foundation of the earth (Revelation 13:8). This is also why we see Jesus visiting Abraham when He came to see the cities of Sodom and Gomorrah (Genesis 18). Jesus made many "pre-incarnate" visits throughout Scripture. These would be more accurately titled "outside of time" visits because they are only "pre-incarnate" according to our calendar. Jesus can move in and out of the timeline as He wishes.

When we speak or declare something it can be moved back and forth through space and time where needed. This is why the enemy tries to keep the right people from speaking and why he tries to censor what we can say. When there is censorship there is demonic strategy afoot. In the spirit realm, words are currency that move things from place to place, from time to time, and from person to person. It is only with the currency of words that either angels or demons can operate.

In the spiritual realm there is also not the limitation of space because it is not bound by the laws of physical distance. I can speak from my living room and declare or command something to happen and it will instantly go forth in the spirit realm. This happens whenever a believer speaks regardless of who they are or what position they hold. This is what every believer needs to do and can do. You do this by believing Jesus' words and declaring His words boldly from your spirit.

This is how I operate in my daily life. When God shows me something I command strongholds to be taken down or speak into the situations over countries, cities, or individual lives. This should be the normal mode of operation for all believers not just those who see in the spirit realm. However, to operate in this way we must first believe that it is possible and secondly understand how it works.

# WALKING IN AUTHORITY

I recall a specific time when I walked into a restaurant with my family. As we entered the foyer and walked towards the counter, I saw two large demons each over 6 feet tall flanking either side of the hostess. The poor woman had no idea. I knew that the demons were positioned at the entrance of the restaurant to prey on people who walked past them. I looked each demon in the face letting them know that I could see them. In unison they both stepped back against either side of the wall, bowed their heads, and folded their arms behind their backs so my family and I could pass. This is what spiritual authority and weightiness looks like. A greater authority - Christ in me - had walked into the room and the kingdom of darkness had to recognize it.

Why didn't I have to say a word for the demons to move out of my way and to take a submissive posture? For the same reason Christ didn't have to say a word before demons began crying out and begging for mercy. Satan is a spiritual being. As such they can see your spirit man. When you walk into a room any demons or angels present know who belongs to God and who doesn't. They can also see mantles and anointings that people carry. This is why the enemy will attack certain people and not others.

Everywhere I go I am flanked by the hosts. When I went into that restaurant with the two demons standing inside the foyer there were members of the host on either side of me. When the enemy sees a Christian who has the hosts of heaven with them they know that they are dealing with a Christian who understands operating in Christ's authority. We can invite the army of heaven to be our weapon, to operate on our behalf, to tear down strongholds, and to lay the groundwork for revival in cities.

**OPEN MY EYES**

Seeing in the spirit realm is a great asset and weapon for the body of Christ. If you want to see in the spirit realm God can open your eyes like Elisha's servant who saw the hills full of horses and chariots of fire (2 Kings 6:17). These were the hosts of heaven.

I pray and release to you the ability to see in the spirit realm in Jesus' name! You can pray: "Lord, I ask you to open my eyes to see in the spirit realm. I receive this same gift that you operated in while on the earth and that the first Adam had. Thank you for opening my eyes. I look forward to working with you on this new level."

## Chapter Takeaways:

- God is outside of time and is therefore not bound by time. Time operates only in the physical realm.
- In the spiritual realm there is no time or distance.

# 5. THE ARMIES OF HEAVEN

"Don't you realize that I could ask my Father for thousands of angels to protect us, and he would send them instantly?" - Matthew 26:53, NLT.

## PSALM 103

We are designed to be God's companions. God literally made His own friends - you and I. The only One above mankind is God (Psalm 8:5). In the Hebrew text of Psalm 8:5 the word translated "angels" is actually "Elohim". This means we are made below God not below angels. We are the highest order of beings that God created and we are designed to rule with Him. This is why a rogue angel wanted Adam's position in the garden.

The order of creation is:
- God

- Humans
- Angels

People often forget that we will judge angels (1 Corinthians 6:3). The angels are the servants of God but we are the sons of God. As His children, we choose to serve and to work in the family business called the Kingdom. We work and cooperate with the angels and hosts of heaven to do our Father's will on the earth.

When working with God's spiritual beings we must differentiate between their functions to be effective in prayer and when commanding in the spirit realm.
Psalms 103:20-21 (NASB 1995) differentiates between angels and hosts:

> Bless the Lord, you His angels,
> Mighty in strength, who
> perform His word,
> Obeying the voice of His word!
> Bless the Lord, all you His
> hosts,

You who serve Him, doing His will.

The word for "angel" in Hebrew is *malak*. It means "messenger"[1]. The angels or messengers of God act and do His Word. The word "host" in Hebrew is *tsaba*. It means "army"[2]. The army of heaven acts on God's will. Scripture clearly delineates these two different spiritual categories.

- Angels act on the Word of God.
- Hosts act on the will of God.

Jesus is the Lord of Hosts (Jeremiah 31:35). He commands the armies of heaven. Jesus said that the Father could provide Him with 12 legions of angels at His request (Matthew 26:53). Jesus also said that whoever believes in Him would do greater works than Him (John 14:12). If Jesus is the Lord of hosts and commands the armies of heaven, then whatever He can do we can do also and even greater.

# ENGAGING THE ARMIES OF HEAVEN AS A WEAPON

The Word tells the story of David and Goliath. It is one of the most popular stories about warfare in the Bible. David said to Goliath, "[...] I come to you in the name of the LORD of hosts, the God of the armies of Israel, whom you have defied." - 1 Samuel 17:45, NJV. David knew the power of calling on the God who commands the heavenly army. He also knew that the true army of Israel were not the men too afraid to approach Goliath but the unseen armies of God. David knew that the real weapons were the hosts. This is something that has been lost today.

David's weapon was his voice and his understanding of Scripture. The slingshot was the physical representation of the spoken Word. Our voice is the offensive weapon. David made a declaration in the spirit realm about who his God was and that he was going to kill Goliath. This destroyed the demonic powers of intimidation and darkness operating in the Philistines which manifested in a physical victory.

Speaking and commanding in the spirit realm is often the most difficult thing for Christians to do. Most people - like myself - feel somewhat uncomfortable with speaking out loud at first. When you speak out you are engaging the Sword and actually putting it to use. You are also engaging the spirit realm. Witches know this but God's own people don't. When we stand up to engage an enemy an entire army is behind us backing us up as we go.

The army of heaven wears actual armor and has actual weapons. I have had them show up at my work and in my home on different occasions. When I travel they are with me sitting on top of the plane. Some of them look very intimidating. This is probably why when the hosts declared the birth of Christ the shepherds were terrified (Luke 2:8-15). The shepherds looked up and saw an army of warriors singing at them in the sky.

# HOW DO WE COMMAND THE HOSTS OF HEAVEN?

Here is a quick synopsis:

- Invite the hosts of heaven to be your weapon: Repeat after me: "I invite the hosts of heaven to be my weapon." The Lord has now given you members of the army to command.
- Take power over the enemy: To command the hosts you have been given, say "I take power over all power of the enemy." When you do this you are asserting the authority Christ has given to you. The army of heaven does not have power over the enemy because that authority has only been given to God's people.
- Command the hosts: Command the hosts to take down demonic strongholds and platforms over the lives of people and places. Say, "Hosts of heaven, take down

every demonic stronghold, shred every platform, and demon in my neighborhood." You can command this same thing over people's lives and regions of the world.

- Daily Prayer of Protection: Say, "Hosts of heaven, protect me and my family. Protect us from all accidents and injuries. Protect us from all attacks both physical and spiritual." This is something I say everyday.

**You are never too young or too old to command the hosts of heaven. This is an authority given to all believers because Christ our Lord is the commander.**

Resource: I encourage you to check out Prophet Kat Kerr. She is a seer who has amazing teachings on commanding the hosts of heaven. The Lord gave her the Host Initiative. You can find her resources at https://www.revealingheaven.com/. You can also find videos on her Youtube channel https://www.youtube.com/user/TheKatKerr. These resources have been very helpful to me and taught me many things.

Before I go into a place or a city - even when I first wake up in the morning - I take power over all the power of the enemy. I command the hosts of heaven to protect me and my family everywhere we go. When I go into a place that I know has demonic strongholds or oppression I command the hosts to go before me and to destroy the enemy and to tear down his strongholds over people, places, cities, and regions. They will do exactly that. I have seen 3 to 4 hosts lay hold of one demonic spirit and literally tear it apart.

Several months ago I was praying for someone who had been under attack. As soon as I started praying, I commanded the hosts of heaven to surround and to protect the individual. The Lord then told me to point at them by waving my arm in the air. This made zero sense to me but I did it anyway. I then turned and saw two members of the host coming into the church. They were looking side to side. As soon as they saw me pointing at the person they ran over to where we were and surrounded them on either side. This is what happens in the spirit realm when we assert the authority that Christ has given us and obey what He tells us to do.

On another occasion I was in church on a Wednesday night. When I walked in and sat down I saw an angel standing in the corner of the room behind me. I kept turning around and looking at him wondering why he was there. Towards the end of church a small demon spirit flew right into the room. Since I was sitting in a group of people I didn't want to announce abruptly that there was a demon in the room. In my mind I prayed, "Father, please tell that angel to take care of the demon." Before I even finished my thought the angel lunged forward to the right of me and grabbed the demon. The angel picked up the demon like it was a chew toy. It screamed and tried to get away but was powerless to do anything.

## ANGELS

There are angels for different assignments. When we speak the Word they act on the Word. Multiple types of angels and spiritual beings exist and are mentioned throughout Scripture. Isaiah 63:9 mentions the angel of His presence saving the afflicted. There are angels who are ministers of finance. There are also angels of glory. This angel has shown up in my living room. This angel looks like a cloud of glory. As you look deeper into the glory cloud you can see what looks like a man standing in the midst of it. From this angel's face flows the glory of God like waves of water. This angel is linked to revival and will often be assigned to people who have an assignment to bring revival into a city or region.

People also have personal angels. Matthew 18:10 tells us that children's angels are always before the face of the Father. People are assigned personal angels. I have seen mine and have seen other people's. Personal angels do not engage in spiritual warfare like the hosts, but they are there to help us accomplish our destiny. If you have ever been going down the road and heard a very clear and loud voice in your head saying, "Stop!", "Slow down!", or "Turn right" you have heard your angel.

You listened to that voice and realized later that you avoided a deadly accident. Everyone has an assigned angel(s) whether they are saved or not. This is why both Christians and non-Christians alike will have similar experiences in this regard.

### Chapter Takeaways:

- **God made man for Himself to fellowship with Him. God also made a family to rule and to reign with Him.**
- **Psalm 103:20-21 describes the different functions of angels (messengers) and hosts (army).**
- **Jesus is the commander of the armies of heaven.**
- **As Christ's body we also have the authority to invite the armies of heaven as our weapon to aid us in spiritual warfare and to protect us.**
- **The hosts of heaven can tear down spiritual strongholds, defeat demonic spirits, and destroy platforms that the**

enemy has constructed which permit territorial spirits to rule over individuals, cities, and regions.

# 6. THE SOUL

## WEAPON: KNOWING THAT GOD IS ABSOLUTELY GOOD

"[...] Only God is truly good." - Mark 10:18, NLT.

This chapter is vital. I am going to explain how the soul operates and that we don't have to hold on to life's baggage. I am also going to show you how to get rid of things like fear, shame, trauma, addiction, and anger from your soul. I put this chapter last on purpose. We can know everything there is to know about spiritual warfare but still not know how to get healing for our own souls. Many Christians walk around with wounds and pain.

The soul is not your spirit. The soul is your mind, will, and emotions. It is a part of your spirit man. **Knowing that God is absolutely good is essential to having a healthy soul and perspective. It prevents the enemy from stealing revelation from you. It also protects your soul from**

**developing wounds.** The soul is a battleground area. The Kingdom of God can reside within the soul of a man or a woman. The enemy also wants to put his kingdom inside the souls of people because he is nothing but a copycat.

**You must know that God is absolutely good and that He has not brought any evil into your life.** One of the enemy's weapons is to cause us to believe lies about God.

There are theologies that teach when something bad happens in your life that it is a punishment from God or that God is trying to "teach" you something by hurting you. Why would the enemy want something like this to be taught? Because he knows that if we believe the lie that when something bad happens to us that it is a punishment from God then we will accept it. This causes us to believe lies about God. These lies leave wounds on our souls that the enemy can exploit later.

# THE KINGDOM OF GOD IS INSIDE YOU

Jesus said that the Kingdom of God is within you (Luke 17:21). If a kingdom can dwell in the soul of a man then we know there is a battle over this area because there are two kingdoms to choose from. The enemy tries to deposit things from his kingdom into our souls from things we see and hear. This includes things spoken by other people.

The human soul is designed in such a way by God that it holds the issues of life (Proverbs 4:23). The Hebrew language defines "the issues of life" as a "source", "border", or "boundary".[1] This makes complete sense when we understand the soul the way God does. He sees the soul as a place to hold His Kingdom and to release it into the earth. We are literally God's Kingdom containers. This is why we are called God's vessels (2 Timothy 2:21).

The enemy as an imitator of God seeks to fill people with his kingdom concepts and principles which are nothing but lies and deceptions. This is why he tries to infiltrate news, politics, government, education, and religion. It is an attempt to change people's attitudes and perceptions so that they will not be able to see God and His Kingdom accurately. The enemy tries to get us to receive distorted perceptions into our souls on purpose. This is a tactic to try to steal revelation from us. When we are presented with a distorted version of the truth and we choose to accept it, it opens the door to allow twisting of the Word. When this happens it can be very difficult to identify.

Our adversary wants people to think how he thinks so they will speak his agenda on the earth. We can not give the devil an inch of room in our lives (Ephesians 4:27).

## HOW THE SOUL OPERATES

The soul is made in such a way that it absorbs whatever is around it like a sponge. This would not be a problem in an unfallen world. We were made to live and to saturate in the glory and presence of God. Because there is darkness present on the earth, sometimes the world's thoughts, attitudes, and ideas get into us without us even realizing it. Sometimes it is unavoidable to prevent things from being absorbed. This is why we need to do health check ups on our souls. This is also why we are commanded to guard our hearts above all else (Proverbs 4:23).

Satan cannot attack your spirit because it has been redeemed. Holy Spirit lives inside of your spirit so the enemy goes after the soul instead. The soul realm is where demons seek to wreak havoc. The enemy tries to make you feel depressed, anxious, overwhelmed, stressed, self-conscious, inferior, shamed, etc. He tries to get you to feel a certain way so that you will speak a certain way and put labels on yourself and others. As we know, when we speak our words have power.

One of the primary goals of demonic attacks is to get you to come into agreement with the enemy. This is done through lies and deception. When you believe the enemy's words they go into your soul. I have seen people who have dark spots on their souls. This includes believers. These areas are areas where the enemy has wounded or influenced a person. Examples include self-hatred, condemnation, sadness, shame, regret, and despair. These things need to be released into Jesus' hands. The Lord reveals these things to us so we can get rid of them.

Trauma is something that goes into a human soul.

This includes:
- Childhood trauma such as verbal, physical or sexual abuse; neglect and shame.
- Adult trauma such as PTSD from war; physical or sexual abuse; betrayal.
- Grief from the loss of a loved one.
- Pornographic images.
- Horror images.

The images of things we have seen and the sounds we have heard can be removed from our souls so that they can no longer affect us moving forward.

We are commanded to renew our minds because only a renewed mind can understand the will of God and His good intentions towards us (Romans 12:2).

# SILENCE THE VOICE OF THE STRANGER

I want to make something very clear - struggling in an area of your soul is not a measure of "how good of a Christian" you are and in no way does this affect your salvation. Christians struggle with suicide, depression, and addiction or return to old habits. It does not make you less of a Christian. It just means that we need to use the tools available to us to drive out the darkness that is coming against us. The thoughts and feelings that people experience are often not their own but the voices of demonic spirits that they are hearing. When the enemy comes against someone he speaks in the first person "I" not the second person "you". This is why so many people believe that the enemy's thoughts are their own.

An important part of guarding our hearts is silencing the voice of the stranger (John 10:5). Jesus said that we will not follow the voice of the stranger. That doesn't mean that sometimes we can't hear the stranger. As believers we have the authority to say, "I silence the voice of the stranger. I declare over myself that I will not be able to hear the stranger's voice." You will find that this stops a lot of interfering thoughts.

## SOUL CHECKUP

"Truly I tell you, whatever you bind on earth will be bound in heaven, and whatever you loose on earth will be loosed in heaven." - Matthew 18:18, NIV.

Most people should probably go through all the things listed even if they have not directly struggled with that particular issue. As we go through life things happen to us that both affect and influence us whether we realize it or not.

Darkness can also come in through what we are exposed to.

It is a good idea to make this a common practice in your life and to do it on a frequent basis for your soul health. Some people may not feel anything and some people may feel like a new person. This practice isn't about what you feel. It's about the fundamental truth of speaking and declaring using the authority Christ has given us. It is an offensive weapon in our arsenal. Please use this list as a guide but also tailor it to your individual needs or to things you struggle with as the Lord directs you. I have seen great results doing this myself and I continue to do it on a regular basis.

**Say, "I loose from my soul in the name of Jesus [Fill in the Blank]."**

**Examples:**

- Fear
- Shame
- Regret
- Abuse

Worry
Human opinion
Stress
Unforgiveness

- Pain
- Anger
- Bitterness
- Envy
- Depression
- Perversion
- Addiction
- Deception
- Self-Hatred
- Suicidal Thoughts

Strife
Jealousy
Anxiety
Rejection
Manipulation
Witchcraft
Trauma
Death
Insecurity

- Evil words spoken to me or against me
- Ungodly soul ties and emotional connections
- Lies spoken to me or that I have believed
- Darkness and demonic influence
- Evil images I have seen or evil sounds I have heard

I would also add at the end, "In the name of Jesus I choose as an act of my will to close any doors to the enemy or to the kingdom of darkness over my life".

Note: If you find that you struggle with unforgiveness do not wait until you "feel" like you can forgive that person. Forgiveness is not a feeling but a choice. If you know that you need to forgive someone, say "I choose as an act of my will to forgive [name]". When you do this you are making a proclamation in the spirit realm that you have forgiven this person. It may take some time for the rest of your soul to catch up. This is why Jesus made forgiving those who have wronged us a part of the prayer that He taught His disciples. Matthew 6:12, NLT: "[...] forgive us our sins, as we have forgiven those who sin against us". Jesus knew the power of saying that we forgive those who have wronged us out loud.

Once you have loosed things from your soul that you no longer want you always add or bind back to your soul things that you do want. You have given Jesus the garbage so now let's invite the light. When you dispel darkness you always replace it with the truth.

Say, "I bind to my soul in the name of Jesus [Fill in the Blank]."

Examples:
- Life
- Peace
- Stability
- Joy
- Patience
- Restoration
- Favor
- God's identity for me
- God's approval
- The love of God
- The heart of God
- The light of God
- The Word of God
- The goodness of God
- The opinions of God
- The mind of Christ
- The Kingdom of God
- Boldness for the Lord
- The destiny of God

Faith
Forgiveness
Holiness
Righteousness
Kindness
Purity
Truth

- Health and wholeness

Add whatever else to the list that you want or feel that you need. You literally choose who you are and the type of person you become by what you bind to your soul.

**Resource: I encourage you to check out Prophet Kat Kerr. She is a seer who has amazing teachings on loosing things from your soul. You can find her resources at https://www.revealingheaven.com/. You can also find videos on her Youtube channel https://www.youtube.com/user/TheKatKerr.**

# WHY THE SOUL EXISTS

The soul operates on relationship. This is how we are wired by God. Relationship is revelation. A deep relationship with Christ is based upon revelation of who He is. When we speak from revelation we are speaking from a place of relationship that the devil cannot reach. There is a dividing line coming between those who operate from knowledge and those who operate in revelation. The presence or lack thereof of evidential power will be seen.

The soul is designed to commune with God. We are the only creatures hardwired for God to be His companions. (Genesis 1:26-27). The soul is the deepest part of a human being made up of the mind, will, and emotions. The way our souls are wired is part of what makes us like God and what differentiates us from the rest of creation.

## WHAT A SOUL LOOKS LIKE

The Lord showed me my own soul. The soul looks like a cylinder or a column inside of your spirit man. The soul extends from the top of your chest to the bottom of your torso. Scripture talks about the distinction between the soul and the spirit in Hebrews 4:12, NKJV: "For the word of God *is* living and powerful, and sharper than any two-edged sword, piercing even to the division of soul and spirit [...]". The soul and the spirit are separate and distinct. Sometimes people confuse the two as being one in the same.

Inside of our souls are our destinies, giftings, and callings. God will also place things inside of our souls that we need for our lives. I often see words written on other people's souls that God has placed there. They are always good words. They sometimes relate to a particular gift such as healing that God has given them to use for His glory.

This is why the enemy wants access to the human soul. Our souls are wired in God's likeness and his is not. Yes, satan has a soul and so do all spiritual beings or they would have no mind or will to make decisions with. As we discussed earlier - one of God's images is needed to influence and to exact change in the natural realm. Satan does not have the legal right or authority to exact change in either the spiritual or physical realms. This is why he must go through a human being to do it because only we have the legal right to operate at this level.

# THE SOUL OF CHRIST

Jesus stated that "[satan] has nothing in Me] - John 14:30, NKJV.  What does this mean? It means that in Jesus' soul there was nothing of the enemy in Him. We all know Jesus was sinless, but He was also whole in His mind and in His emotions. Jesus was betrayed, accused, and slandered throughout His life, but He did not permit it into His heart. Jesus guarded His soul from the words of men and from the words of the enemy. The Lord filled Himself with what He saw His Father doing (John 5:19) which made Him unshakeable and unbreakable. Jesus knew that He could trust His Father no matter what happened because He is absolutely good.

God is bringing His people to the same place of intimacy that Jesus walked in with the Father. He is wanting all to experience this. God knows that when we are in His presence and are saturated in His glory that all things are healed and made new.

Old attitudes wash away. We see God in a new way. We have more accurate perception. Use the tools that God has provided to you and abound in the joy of His presence. It will make you unstoppable. There will literally be nothing that you cannot do.

## Chapter Takeaways:

- **The human soul was designed to commune with God because it reflects God's own soul.**
- **The soul houses your mind, will, and emotions.**
- **The soul resides in your spirit man but is distinct from it.**
- **Our souls are where our decisions and choices about life are made.**
- **What we believe shapes our soul and creates a filter through which we either accept or reject information.**
- **God places good things about us including our gifts and destiny in our souls.**

- The soul absorbs whatever it is exposed to, whether good or bad.
- Christ walked on the earth without allowing anything from the world to get into Him. He lived with a completely whole soul.
- Because we live in a fallen world our souls can retain negative events, traumas, bad influences, and cruel words spoken to us. God has given us the ability to use the power of our declaration to loose bad things from our souls and to bind the good things of God to our souls.
- Soul loosing and binding should be a regular practice and part of guarding our hearts.
- Part of spiritual warfare is first mastering yourself.
- Give your soul the intimacy with God that it needs. Invite Holy Spirit to help you practice intimacy with Jesus and the Father. Intimacy with these 3 will make you invincible and unstoppable. You will be taught revelation and mysteries that

you did not know. Revelation marks you for life and imprints itself into you. It is literally giving God more of your soul to use for His Kingdom.

- With God nothing is impossible.

# NOTES

Chapter 3: Speak

1. "Οἰκοδομέω." Bill Mounce, accessed 28
December, 2021.
https://www.billmounce.com/greek-dictionary
/oikodomeo.

Chapter 5: The Armies of Heaven

1. "4397. Malak", Strong's Exhaustive
Concordance, Bible Hub, accessed 28
December, 2021.
https://biblehub.com/hebrew/4397.htm.

2. "6635. Tsaba", Strong's Exhaustive
Concordance, Bible Hub, accessed 28
December, 2021.
https://biblehub.com/hebrew/6635.htm.

Chapter 6: The Soul

1. "8444. Totsaah", Strong's Exhaustive Concordance, Bible Hub, accessed 28 December, 2021. https://biblehub.com/hebrew/8444.htm.

Printed in Great Britain
by Amazon

29428531R00051